Footfalls of the Unknown

poems by
Richard Taylor

Goose River Press
Waldoboro, Maine

Copyright © 2020 Richard Taylor

All rights reserved. No part of this book may be reproduced in any form without written permission from the publisher, except by a reviewer who may quote brief passages in a review to be printed in a newspaper or magazine.

Library of Congress Card Number: 2020933534

ISBN: 978-1-59713-213-8

First Printing, 2020

Cover photo by Sally Taylor

Cathedral drawing (page 51) by Mattie Templeton

Published by
Goose River Press
3400 Friendship Road
Waldoboro ME 04572
e-mail: gooseriverpress@roadrunner.com
www.gooseriverpress.com

Poems here previously published

"A Band of Children Marching," *Ice River*, 1987
"Echo Taps for Father," *Goose River Anthology*, 2017
"East of the Divide," *Goose River Anthology*, 2017
"Splicing a Line," *The Café Review,* October, 2018
"Pruning Time," *The Café Review*, October, 2018
"Riding Lesson," *The Café Review*, October, 2018
"Mendelssohn's Bicycle," *The Café Review,* October, 2019
"A Scrap of Paper," *The Café Review*, October, 2019

for Caleb and for Christian

Table of Contents

I The Advent of the Forgotten

The Owl Happens Upon Minerva	1
Soliloquy	3
Echo Taps for Father	5
Apple Tree Dreams	6
Train at 2 AM	7
A Scrap of Paper	9
Sitting for a Portrait	10
Splicing a Line	11
Eric in English I	12
From Old Boy Blue to Young Miss Gabriel	13
Ada at the Nursing Home Interviews a Visitor	14
Opening 1	16
Opening 2	17
To the Mills Downstream	18
Breaking Ground	19
Pruning Time	21
Fame	23

II Up Through the Feet

Up Through Your Feet	27
Wandering Italic	28
Running With Walker	30
Mendelssohn's Bicycle	31
Riding Lesson	32
In the Full Moon Turn of Season	33
Gathering	34
Spring	36
Storekeeper	37
Witness	39
East of the Divide	40

Table of Contents

III The Missing String

What Comes of Giving I	43
II	44
III	45
Something I Can't Remember	46
Tree Line	47
Fireflies	48
Logger	49
Nefertiti Comes to Dinner	50
Reverie in Chester Cathedral	51
Madonna on Bus 28	52
Narcissus Wakes at Seventy	54
Growing Up on the Farm	55
Garden Kiss	56
Not Looking Quiet in the Eye	57
To a Lady Suddenly in Slippers	58
Love on Two Feet	59
On the Trail of a Hip-Casted Texan	60
Cigarette Girl	61
Clown in Love	62
Spicing Life	63

IV A Various Church

Surfacing	67
The Notion of a Bell	69
Dedication	71
A Band of Children Marching	73
Oliver Plays the Flute	75
April 16th	77
Playing Chicken	79
Bill's Thoughts	80

Table of Contents

Laura Taylor's Halloween	81
Graduation Address	83
Hughey and Danny	85
David in Left Field	86
Rachel in Spring Time	87
Pear Tree	88
A Manual of Burying	90
Afterlife	91
A Nice Line	93
April's Letter	94
A Tramp's Odyssey	96
Antique Nails	98
Elegie from Ballyclare	99
Communion	100

I

The Advent of the Forgotten

The A of the P

The Owl Happens Upon Minerva

Feathers filled with blue-black
quiet, talons fed
on gossipy feet,

I float homeward
in half-sleep, sated
and forgetting.

Clouds dim dawn awake, mist
veils every meadow
and woods.

A far barn wants
my closed eyes,
folded wings,

but a shadow below
curls the ribbons of mist
to limbs

lifting a gossamer lady
along a taciturn
dirt road,

and a great tree raises
its crooked hand that I
should wait

on its low branch, look back
over my shoulder,
the way I do—

it is Minerva gliding
in silver light, her laconic
footfall hinting

I might catch her eye
and try to remember
one or two

of the thousand things
she expects me
to know.

Soliloquy

I've long rehearsed but not yet learned
the lines I'd say upon a stage, a monologue
on vagrant miles, fitful sleep,
the reticent stars.

The airy street looks in, all ears
for rapt soliloquy, shifts foot to foot, uneasy
with an actor halting for his script to enter
from the wings,
                    when memory slips in
a syllable whispered by a summer tree
and takes an aisle seat.
                        I start again, but a cavernous bass
within vast overalls and beard shows up to warn me
of tomorrow's thunder and required rain, sits down
a row below to bide his time
and mine.
           An instant turns up by itself, no origin
or end, respectful of another to be partial,
brief, no claim upon a mind,
                            but much upon a pause
to let a whiskered ragged graduate of streams
praise anew the mystic flex his fly rod knows
to show a fish his love,
                        as surely as a wandering strand of hair
curls toward me just as once
upon a breeze from Queen Anne's meadow
dressed in lace.
                The door ajar, a small blond boy
runs in and out and in as if still possessed
by his electric hair and sits down front row right,
                                    (continued)

stalls talk as years ago with his pure
rifle-barrel eyes,
                     while soft upon that nervous air
a fragile hand spreads lean and luminous
across her open book and lends again her minutes' nap
to my beleaguered tongue,
                     just as another once-loved
eye opens close by and lavender, and with its raised eyebrow
silences the spaces,
                     except the graying alto
with a coffee cup leans to her dear friend
and swoons once more for her new shower nozzle
dans le bain,
                     while the bent old woman in black
raises anew her affectionate index finger to instruct
the handsome policeman keeping watch
over her crossing by night
and by day,
                     and I take her hand to an open seat
in their trim garden of trivial events, talkative people
comfortable as stars, perennial
as blossoms.

Echo Taps for Father

I steal from my bed to the top of the stairs
when the lights turn down in my bedroom
and his banjo tunes to the shade
beneath his smile.

I find my balcony seat in high half-view
of the stage below. Softly he sings
things a shadow only says to the fingers
of a calloused hand

to smooth the halting syncopations
of his haying days, lift his late diminuendo
into melody and soothe the night with the lilt
of his long company.

Now whenever my light turns off
I take my seat at the top of the stairs,
and I call back to him.

Apple Tree Dreams

Dreams sleep in an old apple tree, hollow some
and gnarled as the old man, they said, who sat most days
on a wooden bench at the Village Store,

his garrulous universe so loud with the thousand things
he knew, he no longer spoke. In earshot
of its wrinkled bark an apple tree might still

say how a boy could settle with darkness
on its own terms, a bed of boards and a burlap roof
spanning three good limbs. I spread my blankets there,

and the dark came on in the meadow's mist, though no breeze
waked the still leaves, no lithe animal stepped inquisitive
through the high grass, no night bird

asked my name. Only the old man on his daylong bench,
he came. I went to the tree to reckon with night,
and saw the shadow's eye afraid

of growing less familiar with an old man's claim
to infinity's hush. Then it rained, the dark
shed gentle tears as I lay waiting, dressed naked

in my blankets, which I gathered up towards midnight,
knowing little more of the middle earth
of apple trees, and walked back to the house.

In the morning I went to the old man's bench
and sat with him at the Village Store, waking
to the quiet of his day.

Train at 2 AM

He must have got his whistle from a coyote
calling home the moon, more likely from the geese
who know their way around a cloud at night
and fly their choral arrows
north and north,

for that is how he signals to the bed springs
just beneath my head gone bruised
with whips and ragged branches
in a dream.....

         ..... on a twisting thicket path turned
highway cutting on the bias through a pasture
of advancing big-eyed cows, angling
to an antique village street, where a boney gardener
plants silence in my mouth and says to chew the roots.
Ladies in gray bonnets look the other way
and eat pink blossoms from a row of trees, then headlong
strike their faceless voices polyglot percussive
on the glassy air and chase me
down a grassy lane to an endless fresh white-painted porch
with tiny windows and no door....

                              .... when from a distance
down the line infectious harmonies of iron
touch my springs and tell me I have time enough
to catch the 2 am through town to places out of mind.
Of late I take the straight and narrow with its well-connected,
        well-conducted
messenger of crossings, climb aboard the alto signal
of his mellow saxophone caught musing with the moon and
        wings,
hoots news both indecipherable and certain that we fly
above the clouds beyond the nicks of time, the doubts
of love. I ride the singing of the geese who take me flying
north by north to feathered bedding
and untroubled sleep.

A Scrap of Paper

What ruin is a random hand
across a remnant page, crumpled
in a corner of his writing shed floor?

The penman sent his gang, partial words
all angles to the page, pushing,
tumbling like children out the door
and none of them a name.

You've only found him rowdy
in his heart's weather and salt breath
tossed wet and torn with sea sound,
and furtive prayer.

He knew a name was just
a place to flee with the riddle of himself
close by his side until they danced
the very curl of fingers
into words

cursive with self that comes
to those who now and then will start
alliterating with a glib unfinished wind,
answering its questions
not yet asked.

Being comes hungry, catches a man foot-sprung
and giddy, scribbles left behind
and safe no more.

Sitting for a Portrait

It won't be art if my name tags along,
the uninvited guest who knows too much, wraps dreams
in riddles and rhyme, jealous of an artist loving
a canvas not yet done,

the way a cozy hillside famous for its name
declines to speak as bedrock to my footfall or admit
it stills its thirst at a subterranean spring

where an artist might assume her ease
in the shade of talkative trees, or a painted lady
folded in her wings beneath a leaf at night
might dream of the sun's sudden touch
or a thistle's blue perfume,

where she might also catch the dance
of children sparked from the unturned earth
into the arc and aim of birds.

Who else would burn in their thin flame, struck
by an arrow of light, announced without bell or bark?
It's a fire volunteer who hears the latent ring and races
toward places unbeknown, hand in the hand
of a tugging breeze

or the patient rain brushing an exposed ledge
with its fresh news until an ink descends
from the closing light

to a stone split off by long frost, the fit
of an ample hand and enough to wedge a stuck door open
to the chance encounter with an unattended self
sitting in a chair.

Splicing a Line

Pause a moment, the half thought twisting
like a rope lying limp across your hands. Unravel the strands
a hand back from the end, backtwist

into the rope's own turn a hand back more.
Go through with the fid, pry wide for the middle strand
to find a way back into the open rope.

Snug the center strand there, and an eye
begins to open. With the fid again open the next arch
and pass the left strand through, then the right

on its own side. Back twist, open again, thread under
and over the original twist, again and again
until the loose strands run out.

Trim the ends and roll the rough braid
beneath your foot, back and forth, until
the weave smooths, the spliced eye rounds.

Long enough at sea, now it's a pen that pries against
the twist of thought, threads the strands across the turn of phrase
and opens an eye for what I am looking to say.

Eric in English I

The question hits his head
like a thicket of bushes, and birds burst
chirping to each other, flying off
in all directions first, then gathering
in front of the mouth again.

His eyes wander,
for the surprise is great, the joy
that the flock of words rides the air
so easily, so smooth.

Can I get them all to fly together in a line
and back to me again? he asks himself,
and with a chin wedge notched for a narrow mouth
and whistling: Can I sing my thoughts back too?

Do the brows leap over my eyes
like boys over a puddle full of sky? For I would like
to see what fills the air more comfortably and find
how a bird flies, one bird, or two, or sings
one note, two notes, or three.

From Old Boy Blue to Young Ms. Gabriel on Blowing the Horn

How may an older fellow man
advise such a Gabriel lady and yet
not totally consent

to say that what she is saying
is really saying it? The question
after all, is too formal, except

for roguish approximation as in poetry,
or as 4 is to 5 if they are just together
and not yet reversed.

Your notes sound out
so angular and warm, chiding concepts
like children giggling at clarion parents.

It's better when the connections get closer,
when the words bump into each other and become
good friends without the early prejudice

of thought, and full of surprise at starting out
strange bedfellows. Let the words fit
and hold, by smile or wink or tear

or fear, you have no choice
but to wager. What grows follows
a good tilling—more than telling—

dirt words, and grammar
is an old farm tool.

Ada at the Nursing Home Interviews a Visitor

Black caps and red vests, skinny legs and those big feet
turned out, feathery skirts - they come to my feeder,
you see.

They're comfortable around my eyes, the blue gone pale
with forgetting. They already know nothing's old,
nothing new.

Thirty-four years of room 8 at Rumford Elementary
was such a lovely flurry of wings.
And who are you?

No pigtails and bangs, no big ears
and black cap, a red vest pocket,
feather stripes?

Are you the shy whistler in seat five,
perched little but hoping to be heard, the buff wren
in my back yard?

She comes to the fence post there, you see,
scolding you here with me. You say
we were six

and we chewed a single stick of gum, you then me
then you then me, behind your porch on Harlow Hill.
Oh then, you are Laura,

and we were six, and didn't we talk all afternoon
like catbirds hiding in the honeysuckle,
such a good tangle

of leaves and twigs to sit together nicely. Hear the pair
there now, chatting as they do
how red berries

put sweet in our wings, so we fly away
like lace unraveling on the narrow air
where all our secrets go.

Opening 1

When will come the opening, the doe sleep
in a common sun or run
unhurried in her smile?

Then in a dream dark
a day rises willfully anew
against the given hour, kills the sleep inside
and takes her back to the mystery
of thickets, shelter of riddle, the dare
to touch and mark and leave
unknown.

From the tangle to this gallop
is a joyed leap from query to a clearing
empty of thought. Big in the eye, ears full
of every telltale silence, she gives up
the sprung hidings of suspicion, twitching
with haste.

Opening 2

In the opening place of people, being near
is not close enough, and speaking
does not say.
                Blindfold your words now,
send them out on foot and finger across the hollows
of ground, body and into the errant caves
of fellow creatures timid
in their power.
                A dark caress
shades the timorous palm, uneven softness
teaches the feet to dance their peculiar doings
and forbid a name.
                Go there, not in mere friendship
but alone or in love. Tangle secrets.
Hide the new unknown
in thickets.

To the Mills Downstream

Dear reader, I'm not an old man,
nor young either. Call me seventy-five or so,
around long enough for these poems to stack up
like logs stuck behind the makeshift dam
of unattended years.

January howled at February, February at March
and now it's spring the melt
is getting pushy. The dam begins to quiver
towards noon, as the day warms,
and starts to weep, as they say.

Few notice. One trickle
looks about like another, fingers
of the same hand. They don't hear the head
beginning to bump beneath the ice. The main thing
is not getting their feet wet.

I know better. I've been awash my whole life
and never gotten cold feet, and I'm saying it's time
to burst the dam and let a long season of trees
cut in the high cold run helter skelter downstream
all at once, the whole bunch of them.

Let the mills decide what they're good for—sawlogs,
some pulp—but no veneer. I peeled them hard myself,
first thing. And if you don't believe me,
let me take you into the chill air of a man
who had to love winter.

Breaking Ground

Back from winter in a night
pushing rudely through a spring snow
come late by two feet, quiet comes melting,
is over, is gone well. I wake
for breaking ground,

for I would have the ground
accept my rest, the air my hints
at flight, if down the wind and caught
between old words and dirt, a digger
can bare fresh bones. I would turn
the riddle of a colder season past,
the early cry died in its dweller
before the first good rain. Pale lips
remain, blue above the garden,
yesterday's grave - much to till,
little to eat.

For a week long day each hour fills
of itself, empties my blind hands
scanning words from the eye-worked quiet,
from a kiss cracking my dirt innards
of their chill speech, from fingers
searching the hours for trust
in the perfumed earth.

Where no tracks keep I'll dig,
reach down to pale roots where a thing
abides in its riddle deeper down. Bones
belong so to themselves, move only
as embers to breath.

I'll stir the earth, know soon
if the furtive brush of waking
hints of rain.

Pruning Time

March is pruning time, shears and cutting pole
let in the sky, trim out the shoots that would
outrun the muscled limbs that bear
and bring home apples.

What ritual do I dance, circling the trees?
I'm neither a pious deacon nor a priest but just
a country man, and the old ones show me light
through their innards gaping

brown and damp, dug apart by ardent woodpeckers
hungry for grubs and the sap already climbing up
the lean live wood toward petals for orioles
and September picking.

Time's honed axe has long been busy splitting
down the middle of the wasting trees like a sleepless
woodsman, and he's impatient with our shadows
borrowing the light.

I won't be long, but I must trim
the crowding shoots, the crooked twigs,
as the trees have trimmed me to the ways
and wages of aging.

Planted like me in '38, they see
right through me and know a metaphor
can fashion of a man a givable self,
even on a chill spring day.

They have had their long look at me,
and we cleave as if twinned in the thin sharp
light that looks for heartwood. They have felt
the breath of shears

and cutting pole above the patient snow
and will attest to pruning's wages
paid in apples and a simple man
who plies his gift and skill.

Fame

I've done my best for wings with a pair of feet
and their shoes, and fame finally beckoned
the early afternoon I lighted at the doctor's office
on one shoe red for running, the other brown leather
for town and was too gently welcomed by a sturdy nurse,
her universe of eyes looking down
with sudden deity, her
infallible smile.

Once upon a time I climbed Olympus
and watched immortals racing radiant from battle
to bower, bacchanals to thunderbolts, but jealous
of heroes, with little left of their endless time
for fitting feathers to mortals.

The gods are also wise to mundane lives
and leave celestial nominations to the Fates. One of them
this nurse, Lachesis surely, stepped forth from the labyrinth
to set the length of her stern ruler by my frayed thread,
assess the chances on my own two feet, and
remember me forever,

even though she wouldn't enter in my file
that one shoe felt as fit to wear as any another
when moments before I started for town a phrase
of poetry, sudden and lovely, diverted my concern
for pairs.

Sages and even poets have sometimes said
that fame is not a pretty sight, for solitude soon
tempts a spirit's gift of self with the lush vagaries
of a second shoe.

And how else would the gods have learned
their awful patience if not from fickle history
that forgives us for assigning wings
of our own design?

As for that other shoe, the one lifelong yet to drop
and forever none too soon, it will strike a feathered footfall
for the few who listen, far from the gaze of gods
both great and small.

II

Up Through the Feet

Up Through Your Feet

If an old man told you
the best information comes
up through your feet,
would you walk or run,
and how far?

What will your feet feel
to know where they've been,
become acquainted with an earth
that knows how to be a stone
or a bed of straw?

And how do the earth's syllables
ride like atoms up the blood,
stow away in the heart, pulse
in your finger tips toward
puzzling love?

You only hope in the lift
of a dance or run you'll hark
to the ground's quiver
in your tongue murmuring
something about the universe
not very clear,

even though you've told the truth
about the bright stone stars
lurking in the dirt dark
with something to say
to your feet.

Wandering Italic

I slip from a cave's quiet into the wind's love
and dare the turning earth to bless
and keep me captive. But the wind nudges
off-balance, tilting italic, and I run forth cursive
into narrative with a voice still timid
to have its say.

I have sorrowed how the less loved stumble,
forsaken by crass lamplight on the wet street
they cross, the gloss that erases footprints
in a town that knows everything
and prefers to forget.

So I take to the single mercy of the dark alone
along a dirt road where footfalls temper memory
with privileged talk, the imprints of longing too delicate
to be spoken.

The mild abiding lean and my ambled word attract
the puzzled gaze of faces singing from a cliff
to the indifferent sea. None has much to say
though each is clothed in a soft hymn sung
but to a third or fourth and thence never to pause
within earshot of the wind.

I wear a curious eye, blunt boots, pant legs
taken with dust, a rib cage ringing with half-heard
music where I turn and squirm to the earth's dim drum,
or when the wind visits, baton pointed high,
hear voices flutter like flushed wings
into the evening sky.

My perfect shadow tags along, even into the night,
pleased in vain with the infant syllables of an epic dream.
But after I sleep good hours beside a road apart
or in the arms of a green hill, I keep to my italic step,
its loops and curves, that it may spell some just arrival
among sure-footed words, in gravity's grace to voice my say
before I trip and fall.

Running with Walker

He harks to the bell, drops plane and clamp, and cuts
across the fields, up East Hill, for Swains barn
is on fire, and getting to a fire sets Walker burning.

I chase the soles of his shoes over the pasture grass,
cow flaps and gray ledge, and don't dare let go,
for I am caught and happy in his draft, for he always

runs to where a fire is, a barn, a forest lit by lightning,
blueberry burn for the fallow year, the better to find out
if blowing hot outdistances solitude, riding

the furious draft that drives his bones to raze
the breathless shelter of angle and pitch, curing
sweat with velvet ashes, running incandescent

to a clearing sky. And soon in the tug
of an innocent cloud he imagines a chair
bent round as a rain drop dripping

from an apple branch, a table long as forest shade
and wide as thanksgiving, a maple sheep in wooden fleece
with a smile wider than creation's ears.

Mendelssohn's Bicycle

Mendelssohn is coming down the road
on a bicycle and not with a violin
but with a whistle, though he wonders
would a violin keep up with his feet's
frenzied pedaling, the hill's lift and its dive,
the wind's thin hum in the spokes.

Light fingers of air steal his hair flat back
for wheeling into the earth's own pent-up
hell-bent melody.

He wants to whistle the universe close,
and he lifts his arms like the handlebars
wide, rides with no hands, conducts
the wind lest it turn lazy, the clouds
lest they rest in the trees.

A crescent curve through vast cornfields
turns the belligerent wind to his back
till his bicycle fills like a wishful kite
with gusts of amorous blue.

Over Sawyer's flats to the beach at last,
the cycling boy and his whistle slow, the wheels
concede, lean quiet by the bath house door.

Ripples tripping the water go shy,
the breeze pauses to listen: a concerto in e-minor
leaps from the boy's whistle
into Mendelssohn's ear.

Riding Lesson

"Gallop or get off the horse,"
said the First Sergeant who wasn't,
though there are hills to take with a horse,
and his voice wore chevrons and rockers, three
and three, a loud diamond in the middle that declared
we were all present and accounted for, standing there
in the straw of sunlight kindling
his white hair.

I was to take up the run the horse had
in his hooves, hear them hit the ground
all at once and over and over say time
is forever short, and your only moment
is now; no more waiting afraid of his withers
quivering at thunder and squall out of nowhere
with a name.

His shoulders rolled exultant
over the green knolls, underway
and more, for his feet plucked fine at the turf,
and dactyls and oracles rose from his shoes,
tuning my knees, asking for ears,
quizzing my tongue.

"Short of full-tilt," said the First Sergeant,
"any green field will ever stay quiet. So
give him his head and the meadow will strum
at ease with a boy on a bay at a run. More than that
you don't need, nor even me
to give orders."

In the Full Moon Turn of Season

Afoot at night, wistful as wind
whistling in the pines, my rustling lungs,
I follow the snowed road running.

Crossed loving threw me at the moon
too iced and lucid climbing by, and I go without
some similar feet to bring the light more softly
to my angled path, turn its ice to amber
as on the second day of full.

Muffled feet drum a timid thud
upon the quiet night, caged blood floods
my ribs. Into the quiet trills the river,
running its own ribs, whispers a giant stone
alone in a white field.

Too alive in the fine light, I burst the length
of this night's road to breathe my fill of listening.
Each eye and hand, each leg and my whole middle mass
visit the black wood, the owl calling from a hemlock
hiding in the lift of hills that pull the moon down
to my footfall, my grateful eye.

Voices close upon the speed, each beckoning rock
and tree, the rustle of dry weeds, ice groaning
in a narrow flow, a season's turning song
ringing the night awake, while in the quake of turning
and returning I have softened to the snow, the moon
has guessed my riddle and gentled
my gentleness.

Gathering

    I

So you are cutting basil today
for Timothy, Margaret,
and John, dicing the sunshine to leaves
floating yellow downwind, like runners
on the scent of September herbs. Will you hope
your ducklings into flight so lightly, or your child
onto his first bicycle with your smile
to start his soaring?

If they could simply see your child
burst through the hay field with a fist of daisies, running
a blond and barefoot song to his mother, then would ducklings
fly and friends find wind beneath their feet,
for the ground gives up its gifts to hands
that hide and seek its secret tastes, its softer paths,
hinting we may run for a time with other creatures
and turn our flight to flying.

    II

But that takes practice, said my father,
who long ago in his general store
gathered the Saturday opera to the candy sticks.
He could make pennies and giggling children
chorus of sweets running south, and I among them
a tiny Dutchman, flying fine and finally
in my sneakered mind.

And practice he did, gathering a host of voices up
to choir flight on Sunday! "Then did Elijah the prophet
break forth like a fire!" he sang and sang in all directions
of the taste of mystery, the succor of pain, gathering up
faces blank and similar with hymns and a hushed
first ruffle of wings.

But the time of flying and the run of day
are seldom equal, said he, keeper of bell and clock.
He sang the more because he would but could not fly,
and he set two faces of the church clock
two minutes ahead, saying each of us needs
his own time and will be comforted to know
that if he is going north and south,
he is two minutes ahead of where he would have been,
had he been going east and west. Take your time
in this fickle race, he said, for singing and flight alone
mark start and finish, beginning
and end.

    III

Blessed be you therefore
cutting basil today for Timothy, Margret,
and John, spicing the sun and runners
with a taste of fall. Gather up your child
to soaring, gather up your friends
to hiding and seeking lighter ground, turning flight
to flying, ahead of themselves, but fine
and finally in their own time.

Spring

I could have told you it was spring, had I not forgotten
what reckless joy felt like. But running in the woods,
as we did amidst the wet abandon of single-minded feet,
the joy began to surface like a spring sprung open
from somewhere in the dark ground,
running for a moment but then
trickling away.

It had been too quick to speak of, until
an afternoon in early June, when children
tossed handfuls of pillow feathers
into the wind.

The children all gone home, a swallow
scooped a feather from the grass and chased away, dropped it
in mid-air, and another swallow caught it with a curve,
a climb again, a curl and dive of his own,
or hers.

Fine for a nest, I thought, except
the second swallow spun and dropped the feather
once again, and the first swept in
to catch it.

Since then I have said to myself
it was a spring time when we ran,
and I can say it now also
to you.

Storekeeper

What would a rude and country boy
do with his lover's quarrel with meaning, the fairness
of duty to fruit trees, firewood, a field's distance
within a run, to his fear
of early frost?

Who will complete the season's chores?

Could such a row put an end
to local neatness and the reason
the old storekeeper placed soldier beans
opposite the meat case?

What did he know to set them so?

And coming of age to hunt
the reach of water and warmth, wood
and air, the wordlessness of messages, Paula
at the Fish and Game will talk so matter-of-factly
about the license he will want. But catching her eye
in his shy smile, why would he seek license,
not poaching without it?

Who can presume a license to do?

What would he do, after all, with catch
or conquer or lose, with the quarrel, the dance
of running hot in his huge breath
and puzzling grace? Can a win so rare
not grow faint? How wring the unrelenting
power from losses, enough for him or her or them

(continued)

to gather in the tears that will and should not
be hidden? What certain people shed them,
paying early for the gifts of springs deeper
than dreamed, closer than touched, savored,
suffered, and thus preferred by athletes
tired and excellent with life so totally exquisite
and fatal?

Who will define the rules of doing?

Assemble all things before the storekeeper,
his silence, his space, his fear of the cold:
the wood is thrown in, stacked by size and row, the ice
split out beneath the eves, the snow swept
from stoop and door; bottles, cans and galoshes aligned, stockings
and gloves hung straight beside the lettuce,
oranges and eggs.

How would I do these things, not knowing?

How is a rude and country boy to reason
behind a season's chores and age, set each thing so,
suffer things not so, reckon with rules
and the assumption of license? He has hunted some,
quarreled enough, danced a good deal, run
yet better, endured his win and his loss. He has wept
for many a deeper dream.

It is to do, said the storekeeper,
and you have happened by.

Witness

I see that you are beautiful and floating
over the wide snow, brushing
the white with the hush
of your skis.

On the strings of what idea
are you set free as if a marionette to lift
with skimming earth into
your middle-world of flight and leave
both me and gravity unjealous
as you glide across my eyes,

a smile abiding in the winter air
and nothing more
of you?

East of the Divide, Browning, Montana

Houses of wood and square, sheds close by, lank barns
shrink to spare earth at the river's slow bend.

Wind careens through town, barn boards
bang, gutters rattle, gates slap at their latches.

You can get killed by a flying rock, or trip
on a hard spot in the wind, says a man.

A crow falls across the pale sky, mark of lost memory,
the hush of April, the mountain rushing down.

A Blackfoot girl, trim cut black as a wing, knows
no hurry, marble dark eyes gliding along the gravel street

to her school, lifted in the ruffles of her white skirt.
Her step calms the restless stones and three horses

nibbling thin grass between the churchyard graves
beside her playground with a seesaw.

Dust chases their prints away, and hers
have no need to stay. Her fleet smile turns the air,

murmurs soft song from place to place as breath pleases,
easy as wind from the mountain and April.

She is not late, she is not early.

III

The Missing String

What Comes of Giving

I

I gave you a string
from my violin.
You kept it
and keep it still.

Over old frets
with the same bow,
I hear myself
still playing
the missing string.

I will write poems for you
that are not ours.

II

Failing light
slippered
down the streets
of my eye

and kindled me
to smile
that I could be
tinder to the world's
match,

love struck
on a missing string.

III

The poem
is not ours, though it sounds
when another
happens by,

hears the missing string
ask that we be near

and mute the cruelty
of its solitude.

Something I Can't Remember

I can't quite recall how arms go
around a sudden hug. But neither would an old apple tree
or the honeysuckle remember which green tendrils
go left or right around a hollow trunk, and certainly not
once they've heard birdsong in the branches, or just
a poet rhyming one or two things you didn't know
you knew.

But after the reading you appeared
through the thicket of tweed handshakes,
along with a hug that vanished seconds later. I can't quite
recall it now and doubt I ever will. Memory
would get it wrong anyway, looking where the moment
might have gone, trying to invite it back.

I'd rather be more clear about it,
keeping in mind the honeysuckle and
small birds as I do the swallow that landed
on my hat as I sat by a lake, when the wind went
still, the water turned
emerald.

Tree Line

Eyes at the tree line
see us in the meadow

rolling together in the live hay, wrapped
in daisies and downy clouds forever
fleeing, greeting a green snake
beside his shed skin, curious big-eared mice,
listening to crickets noisy with August love,

or simply holding a kite string
half an afternoon.

Deer are waiting at the trees
for night to open their pavilion of joy
lit only with the most discreet
of stars.

Fireflies

Memory hunts the edge of night, pencil poised
to correct the imperfect draft of self

composed for the calendar's omnivorous smile,
then on a whim seize fireflies for fooling the tongue's taste

for lovers picnicking in places they don't need to know
because what passes between them is not for saying.

Darkness arrives untouched, and love shrinks
to perfection, a flicker of light.

Logger

It's not a decent man
of field or forest will fell
a fair tree roughly, for it
has reached higher and more broadly
than he, held the wind
in its arms in the way
he seeks for himself
and has not known.

Nefertiti Comes to Dinner

It must have been a furious wind that took you
from a sky a world away, even as you land among us
like an exotic butterfly.

In numinous dark blue for dinner, you light noiselessly,
though you might be Nefertiti before the jewels
or gold or immortality.

Your eyes tell more than words of shadows
where the timid world hides in its names,
afraid of loveliness

that makes prophecy too poor for questions
yet unanswered, who your gods might be
or the circumstances

of your creation, for you persuade beyond
what the winds possess, even as you hold to us
like a delicate flower

rooting in cold castle stone, preferring only
to be of this earth.

—for Soraya in Wales

Reverie in Chester Cathedral

How would a novice know that she would sleepwalk
where the dark devours walls and the river of faithful shoes
has worn the floor stones hollow, or know the stones

can tell a rural step is passing by and wake
to the nakedness of her bare feet crossing the chill night
in a dream of heaven's uncut fields quivering

under the wind's great hand? It is a cuddle
far from her father's barn, where as dusk grew dark
she liked to lie on the hay and float in the incense

misting from his sheep and cows, their ruminations
the evensong at day's end. Now in the vacant church
a fragrance from the wooden choir brushes by, a human breath,

and in the trembling air she falls upward in a prayer
of kisses unaccountable for loving everything not there
and never known to the habit's hug or the wimple's white shade.

Now she asks outright of heaven's handsome quiet,
"Are you here, in this high place?" Courtesy delays and dreams
have little time: "And if you cannot answer, let us at least

become love's shape in stone, better yet an open ring of bronze
    whose ends
we look across, if you will walk with me in sleep's garden, wake
    with me
by a fountain filled with lilies, a spring's trickle of water.

By day no one will see us kiss, but they will see it is ordained,
or they will surely guess."

Madonna on Bus 28
After visiting the icon museum in the cathedral in Sofia, Bulgaria

It is a troubling way you lead me, Mary,
and not so easy as riding in on a white horse
to kill a dragon. I wouldn't accept that anyway,
for he is still leashed to a princess, and she
gives no hint of being the virgin given
to this day. St. George killed
and backed away.

Why then do you hold me
so close, when you rest warm and safe
in Sofia's cathedral? Your eyes are painted
on the veined and smoothly muscled wood,
but they see me near and take my naked eyes
without assurance or annunciation
of but a dark devotion in the lover tethered
to a silence, prey robbed of his cry,
a blessing tangled back.

I stand in bus 28 from the city center to the snow hills.
In the rear window the antique sun turns cyrillic stations
inward, riddling Greek: eros, hodigidrea, agape,
kairos.

You stand by the window, bending forward
in the softening afternoon. The brown hair
flows half curls close to the neck. The head
tilts slightly to the side and down. The eyes are brown,
so close to black, limpid in the simple light,
feigning absence, gathering distances,
the shifting of feet.

The icon was right, I will not follow,
for such a one as you will be forever
far away, although so willingly I would
step from the bus and along the mud path
to the dripping trees, into your upturned palms
and folds of blue, into your brown eyes
and their unrelenting
welcome.

Narcissus Wakes at Seventy

Turning from my mirror this morning
I walk out along the few remaining hairs
like tensile strands of fancy on which
to balance and set forth upon
the infinite requirements of my desire.

High above the streets of gab, I step
oblivious and deftly to the company
of clouds, pure white in their abundant
leotards, diaphanous wraps of blue that loosely fold
around three nimbic nymphs who wish me near
to stroke their sunlit cirrus hair.

I stride along the wire of tensed imagining
without a hint of cumulus libido
stumbling profane, for straight ahead I spy
a place to love in gentlemanly circumstance
between myself and the cavalier I feel,
between a thinning ego and
a nicely ripped id,

and from that very opening a lenient angel
breezes toward my mirror's preferential self,
her softest gray-blue eyes for me alone,
and rife with possibility, I think:

if a star infects the dark
with but its single self and so multiplies
its lights, then so might love
in a fresh forenoon.

Growing Up on the Farm

High diddle
diddle the cat
and fiddle the cow jumps
over the moon.

Here I sit
with the cat eyes shooting
the dark all around
a pink moon udder.

I've been here a dozen
dreaming generations, floating
down the Milky Way, skimming
just right,

until that day a willowy
girl stood humming softly,
wiggling her knees in the waves, maybe
her toes in the mud.

That night I looked up
at the moon and said someday
that cow will jump over

to this pasture full of stones, then
the diddle cat will get to drink
and some real milking and fiddling
get done.

Hummingbird

So often has a hummingbird come to the honeysuckle,
I lift a hopeful finger to the blossom's opening

to charm the blur of wings, a shimmer of reds
and greens among the slender petals, pink, pale gold.

His grip tickles like a leaf the breeze, falling
as he folds his wings, is gone,

but is himself self again with lifting from my finger
out of touch with hovering the jeweled

instant on a blossom's lips. I go away-
voyeur, thief, third party to a garden kiss.

Not Looking Quiet in the Eye

I face backwards
to the feral quiet, so it will not be
afraid of my eyes,

kneeling there that you may
inch closer, shy ghost prone
to curiosity

and stroking. Stealthy feet
clear your throat.
I look away

from all desire, that you
may breathe on my shoulder, lean
a little on my back

like a timid animal, not see
my hazel eyes longing
for tenderness,

or the darkness of their error
if I turned to make certain of beauty
coming close

when you only wish to tap my back
with a child's finger keeping time
to subterranean song.

To a Lady Suddenly in Slippers

Postpone this touch, the swiftness of not parting
will sever the league of hands.

Our grip will quicken the crush of fingers
blind with words awry of grace.

Strike tinder away from spark, let the flint cool,
wrapped away in flannel with the steel.

Bed down embedded with the cold of truces
driven between the ribs and hugged to ceasing fire.

Embrace the space between us,
close around it. Hold it large. Conjure in

the open. Start the kiss from far away and walk,
barefoot, across each inch of ground.

Love on Two Feet

Is it even possible
to say the right thing, standing
on your own two feet, manly, balanced, forthright
and calm, hands relaxed, on the hips, or
if need be, in your pockets, as you shift from foot
to foot? You can't help yourself,

although scientists have noted
how you start any step forward
by shifting your weight and balance
to the other foot (for me the left), while
the free foot with the love in it swings into flight, one-legged
with fear, exceeding the limits of stability,
chaos theory would say.

So do it all at once, the shift
and step, quick enough to outrun thought with legs flying
like children chasing a kite, one leg catching
at the ground, the other swinging recklessly
into the air to say "I love you," or
at least to ask "May I have this dance?"

The answer must be: it can't be love
if the two feet belong to the same person,
who will soon know that even requited love
is inherently unstable, as chaos theory would say,
even if the two lefts learn
to do the right thing.

On the Trail of a Hip-Casted Texan

These words for your particular cast
of injured lady let me hope you see
I stumble too (folks from a little state prefer
the larger state of mind). You see my trip,
you say? In my state I have learned
to be not so much lost as bewildered
happily right out of the woodswork,
as you well know. Still, I wonder
if there is enough ink to follow
a Texan's trail. My .44 magnum
pens at my hips, I wager
we'll just shoot it out between here
and Austin. That will decide
once and for all if you and I
are going to be a union or just
a confederacy.

                      A Man from Maine

Cigarette Girl
— an abuse case

You burn with kindness, smile
glowing about your neck.

Your father burns, kindled
with the need to run love
out of bounds, sears a cut inside
along the char of impossible rewards:
he is too big, you too small.

His rage of kindness so refined,
sharpened in an elder's eye to seek
a small girl's smile, burns in the mark
of his embrace along your throat,
the willowed arms that will not take
a father's love within their vapid glow,
his hurt for warmth beyond him, your cry
his love requited.

Clown in Love

A painted face arrives in the light,
gentle limbs spring quick to catch a sigh

heard loud as it falls on faint applause
crippled by eyes and the rush of time to die.

Blood leaps awry, tightens brow and toe,
leaves stomach echoing ache and hope.

The floodlit frown strolls by in shoes too big,
wanders out the cry behind his giant eyes

that ask the audience if you perhaps were held therein.
Could a clown find love more easily outside, he wonders,

a carnival worker in blue shoes, chimney sweep
with no socks but a stove pipe hat that smokes

if you look more closely as he motor cycles with Godiva
snow-white bareback by, rides before the moon

to nod them down to friendly agony when elements
go loving in a vacant cloud floating like an eyelid over,

soft and by. So he'll think of love like a heavenly sage
in sandals, professional of rooftops with no socks,

though his face with shoes so big or so blue won't
turn the moon away from wooing an immaculate sister

down to the cool sand while his painted smile
starves upon her passing into a white sea.

Spicing Life

Mother kept rosemary in the simmer pan
or hung by the door to take the smell of fish
from the kitchen, or father humid
with the itch of stubborn love.

Father knew why and put cloves in a vest pocket
to hide the scent of proper clothes
that oiled his armpits on breezeless days,
as he sweetened the sour corners

of his flesh with his insistent song.
He rehearsed all day for the arms
of night, conceiving melody
in his limbs run damp with scything

by his stone walls, around the apple trees,
singing up and down the scales his
"come and take a walk with me" to comfort
the sun retreating behind the hill.

For sing he could and never cooled
in a cage of words when a good moon rose
to ripple open the darkening waters
of his darlings, defeated heart beats

drumming toward the evening's
waiting serenade, when his honeyed voice
corrected any harmony won cheaply
in a wordy nook of play.

The scorch of love is sweet tomorrow's
ordinary job, he liked to say, and any hymn's
first line, its second rise and shine with noble lust.
The itch will not retire, nor the reek deter

love's joyful sweat for mothers, sons
or lovely ghosts, the rush
to first light's rosy cheek, dusk's
heady softness, gray eyes

waiting at mowing's end,
so long as cloves are in a vest pocket,
rosemary in a simmer pan
or hung by the kitchen door.

IV

A Various Church

Surfacing

I sailed in the mist to a six-month moon, and soon
waves swallowed the sky. Words jeweled
and stolen went down with the ship, the hoard
and its thief.

The bottom got its pirate long sorrowful
for love of women forever beautiful
and far away. How could I suspect
that they would greet me there, nymphs at home
in the depths and clever at pilfering poetry
from a wormy chest to keep as currency
for land where they might cure
from their mute sentencing beneath
the unforgiving sea?

One called my name and said sweetly,
"I had hoped to love you but was afraid,
so caught you were in the spool
of words raveling into nets that tangled you
and spilled your inspirations onto this or that
celestial deck, slithering free as shiny fish
back into their luminous sea. I cried
to watch them go, you with them, my tears
falling inside where the oceans that owned you
would not see and take offense."

Another warned me that any kiss
was as good as a nib, but I've still decided to write,
for I have heard the sounding of an absent son
among the muted voices in the water's clutch,
and I would have them rise to baited words again,
risk the taste for love and doubt the hook. I'll undo
the bottom's suck, and may the mud
come with them.

The souls living in the hoard turn pink
and blink in the blank light, tongues quicken,
the sunk ribs trailing slime breathe green;
the wreckage glows,

while close by in a consonant catch
and the vowel's pull I row, sweeping mist
from a daylit sea.

The Notion of a Bell

So that a voice might be with her, mother loved
and matched her fragile joys with porcelain bells. True
they rang but then soon sadly done, until she favored the bell
from Adderly House, for it had no strike and thus
no pain. "Find it a voice to wake you," she said to me,
"and tell you there is joy."

Yet when I struck the hollow bell
with light iron or stone, the silence
heard none of the rumbling in my veins,
loved only the echo of the Lord's
clarion hours.

Truly I reveled in heaven's ring
but prayed in vain in the village of noise.
No rooftop angel choir sang
to trumpets and to flutes, no rows
of bird soprano song, no virile euphony
of roaring baritones.

But evenings in the shelter of the belfry there
the ringers drilled their ropes to the grip and pull
of syncopated timing in a hymn mathematic
and divine and scaling up and down the throat
of tower wood and stone that pealed against
the shriek of wind, undid gravity with tumult,

tugged me upward to a mother's quiet, while a father's
father's father tolled among the ancient beams, until
in the dusty light a novel tone struck deft
upon the stranger come above.

Then in the village the noise was gone. I spoke
to the rooftop company of my immortal hosts
and matched their fragile joys with phrases
for a mother's centuries of longing, for trialed men
elusive to all following except with sentence pure
and furied in a firmament of words,

for a tethered earth was on my tongue, distinct
and near as breath from out of the hollow night.

Dedication

I hear the fishes sing
the naked music of a stream,
and the water rushes to my ear
in search of news.

I see a bird tip
a tumbling wind, so the wind
may right itself about my feet
in need of passage.

I have heard the chirp
of whales spelling the sea
and sounding the deep, and I
have heard it rhyme

with the elk's pitched whistle
and a bird's note cast
on the wind's dash from cloud
to hilltop and down, from tree
to grass and pond.

So fresh is a curve the fishes give
to the leap of a rhyming stream,
it stirs my son yet small
to patient listening and no question,
floating out beyond himself toward
an indiscernible reply.

A stream, the sea, the wind
in the animals, birds and boys,
to wood and ground, to my small son
I must answer with some measure
of my own to suit their rush and theme,
their curve and dive, their dire
exposing hug.

A Band of Children Marching

the children marching
cannot be the music
that they play,
for the shivered knees

drum the chill
of the winter street
into the backbone
of song. The dewed flutes

of pigtailed girls
drip through the whistled
tune. The thud of bass
and snare of brass

trap notes
inside their rosy cheeks,
and the puffed frost drives
the juggling rows

of tall and short along
the gangling way on wooden
lungs and winded feet until
the hall is reached and all sound

numbs in the dumb cold:
with a crash and bang the drum
and flute and trumpet
and chime are packed away

in cases buckled and strapped. The children
return to giggle and glance,
to smile and huddle,
and shout the unkempt chorus

of knees to run the chill
from a trysting spot, flirting
with whistles, pigtails, shy flakes of snow
in the drifting music of their eve.

–Kuopio, Finland

Oliver Plays the Flute

What breath is it but air
that clothes itself in feathers
and floats upon itself
in birdsong,

or slips the wing
at quiet on a perch
to join the chatter
of leaves conceiving song
within a tree?

It is the wind that whistles
in the granite flutings of a cliff
and cloaks itself
in the folds of a man

whittling and musing
on the smoke that curls
in spirals upward from his pipe,
thinks to hear a rhythm
in the grain

and sets to hollowing a branch,
notching for the scamper and stop
of fingertips that turn the air
to laughter, lullaby and longing

for the absent souls returning
in the call of birds. Of these
is Oliver whose fingers fly
to the caves of wood, and the breath
that is but air

brings forth an ancient boy once more,
and novel song.

April 16th

When we were young, we jumped
into the chill spring stream. It was
April 16th, and the stream at last
was leaping free of ice.

Wild we raced to the broad
black oak to strip our clothes,
for suddenly the earth was soft
enough to squeeze between our toes.

It was to bet the hero
from our dreams to leap
from nakedness to man
before the drive of days

could turn our dares to mud, and quick
to spring the first teeth chattering
those frozen words, melting home
to mother and the sun

to dry the frightened wet
behind our ears before it turned
to dirt. And those were words enough
of water, cold enough of running

pickled premature from
diving into winter, out
to spring, crying out the birth
of heroes, drying into boys,

and then to wonder if all words
and worlds must spring so blue, brave,
leaping into April just to tumble
from the womb.

Playing Chicken

She played her games, could tell
a hard chicken marble at finger flicking
and won every time against two sisters and a friend
who got wet yellow chicken on their flicking fingers,
which was hard to hide for the aroma and made
pointing, which they loved to do,
difficult. Mostly, mother loved
winning.

At first she swung for fun
on the trapeze grandpa made and then the more
when upside down her snow-white bloomers
lit up the barn door and caused boys on tricycles
to gasp, giggle and sometimes crash. Early on
she understood the several ways of skin-the-cats
and somersaults,

but never the way a voice sat down
to her piano and sang. All by themselves
her clever fingers found the softer keys, her bloomers
lit up the barn no more or authored chaos
among young boys. Her skin-the-cats and somersaults
went right inside when his singing
rose from the parallel bars in pianissimos
and pirouettes into the evening air.

Bill's Thoughts

Throw that hat away.
It'd look better on me.

It looks like hell on you.
It's the best I've ever seen.

Do you like your jacket?
It's too noisy for hunting.

I fixed the window you broke.
How'd you know what it cost?

Where'd I hide the key?
I'm good as a barn door.

Do what you're going to do, stay or leave.
Cold should only cost so much.

Will my breathing ever get better?
I walk every day, somewhere.

Where'd you get that hat? they ask.
I tell 'em out west, up north.

Smokey lifts his leg at the granite post.
I shed a tear behind the barn.

Baked beans and rhubarb pie,
I kneel with the Methodists!

Laura Taylor's Halloween

And dressing all in sheets, late
in their forties and full of the daylights, they laughed
and laughed and laughed and ran
at the people all pinched in
for church supper games all Hallows Eve.

I must inform myself again,
she told her neighbor Alice as they masked,
if I will teach my children joy, the inner shriek
at terrible unknowns, giddy
laughter, the chill soak of sorrow
and grief. Ghostlike they must learn

to run, go down where longing
cleans its ache of cold, and then still love
our pale, defiant minister of mystery, salvation
meager as supper, lean as a game.

They must get to know the ghost
a mother and a father, father's fathers
and distant mothers call upon to lift with a stroke of hands
the child too soon too full within,
touched at his beginning with much
softness, chuckle and song.

I listen for the pastor's first word
rather than his last. Listen
how he's pounced upon
by the ghosts behind his eyes when the eve
is theirs. It's his party at the church
tonight, but we'll dress up
white to the grin, tumble and
run and leap, random and merry with rules. Let's go
at the supper games a second time around to hear
his second first word frighten off
his first.

Let's laugh again and call our sons and daughters
forth from slumber, dance them into song,
the cuddle of horror, lovely mischief.

Graduation Address

Do they have any idea
how they are beautiful, these girls
swaying among the graduation guests
like tall grass in the easy breeze
of congratulation?

Are they ready to know
the hints of emerald in their eyes, shy amber
in their smiles that conjure great souls
from the ocean mist, brood upon the danger
of strangers bearing gifts?

An old man might tell them
about the hedge that grows around
innocence, green thorns of a feral heart
that can catch at a muscled sleeve or, if not that,
stall casual attack with an aphasic scratch
and quiet uneasy knees.

Will they convert a common run
on an unsung day to a dance upon melody
sanguine with grace and possession's defeat
at the wind's huge hands?

For it blows forever over their high field
visited by tourists and suitors schooled to statues
where a lady risen from a green knoll and lithe
as the blown grass looks out, turns the land rapturous
and out of reach.

She looks upon a stranger, and he hesitates. Quickly
looking aside, her eyes are yet more beautiful
for the touch of greeting, even though its intent
is a mystery, even though that's not
what was intended.

Hughey and Danny

Two old brooms from the barn
give Hughey MacDonald and Danny Gale
the horses they are looking for to gallop
across the grass, down the hill
to town. One minute they hold their broad-brimmed hats
in the wind, the next slap their bottoms
to urge the horses on.

At the STOP sign by the crossing Danny prances,
rears, shouts "Whoa!" and to Hughey:
"We'll leave the horses here." Patting pistols
at the hip, they advance upon the Village Store,
step resolutely to the counter,
push back their hats.

Menacing with two .44 caliber
index fingers, Danny looks the storekeeper
in the eye. "We're here to rob you! Cough up
two root beer barrel candies!" Feigning fear,
the keeper places two on the counter top. "That's good,"
and Danny nods Hughey toward the door. Backing out,
as any decent robber would, they gallop triumphant
back to barn and porch

and wonder a first time why sweetness
leaves so soon.

David in Left Field
—a baseball player in English class

And it came to pass in the mid-afternoon
that a crack was heard. The crowd arose
and roared.
     And he beneath his baseball cap
reflected casually upon its arc, the idea of it
so clean and stitched, so gently spinning
toward his green, immaculate
domain.
     A move, another move to the left
so light, so fine, dark glasses flipped down
to cool and clear the spheres and with a smile
near debonair command the ball yet far away
divulge its destiny.
             No need to raise a glove,
the literate left fielder drifts gracefully
beneath the flight like a spike-shoed mind flat out
to dazzle the diving word to death and
peg it home.
     No runner this one time
again, but another outrageous
toss!

Rachel in Spring Time

Snow was falling
in a spring day's dusk. A moth flew
fluttering amongst the flakes dancing down
to the ground just warm, now
white again,

and vanished, quick
as a diaphanous dancer suddenly in
from off stage on her own to try
the air for welcome before small music
catches up.

These things I remember but
no path, for no trace stayed
on the white earth, nor was it meant
for following, nor anything but
pale wings dancing
in a brief spring storm.

Pear Tree

This is the first spring
it's flowered.
Six years ago mother
set it there.

Then she started
dying. If it wasn't
one thing, it was
the other — winter
came early, spring late.

Never on time, just like
the rest of us. Buds cracked
where they woke, leaves curled
red in the April freeze.

It is too cold,
too cold, she said,
there are no bees,
no bees buzzing
in the branches.

Sudden with dread
of a chill harvest, she
scolded forth the hum
of summer, while the honey
slowed in her dancer's veins.

Quick, hidden
in twilight wind, a breeze
snatched candle flame
and petal, and she
fell empty in her bones.

Let the season prune it,
she liked to say. Dead limbs
blow away and leave
a way for blossoms.

             —for Creigh

A Manual of Burying

After the ancient custodian
took on burying father, waiting to lift away
the fake grass and do the shoveling
until we'd left, I was alone with him
I had not tucked in as he had done for me
when I was young.

I confessed it to the air,
filled or not as it is with God's kinder breath,
and to the minister who was to help us
bury mother. For her we took to our own shovels
and kept the cold away forever. Music
filled the air as the Good Humor Man
tarried at the cemetery gate, and we all
heard her laugh.

When it came to burying
the minister himself, brother and father,
we knew better yet. We each did a shovel
for fear, another for loneliness, a third for affection
due both him and ourselves, the dirt
with which we come and go. The rest left over
in the wheel barrow his son tipped back
to its own good time and place, sand
no longer hurrying to the narrow opening
of our counted hours.

With gentle feet we tamp and tuck
the green turf trim and square
and say our tempered prayer:
As You have ever tucked us in, Our Heavenly Father,
now let the living hum again the lullaby
of the Good Humor bells.

Afterlife

Among the cardboard cartons Stub lay
serene in his recliner, practicing to die
in his living room by making the effort
to be usual in a world of consignment. It's there
the elements all gather to one's name,
numbered and on a fine day arranged
nearby in an antiques barn for sale to admiring
new owners, for Hope his wife had faith
the afterlife was visiting grandchildren
in California and Alaska.

His logging days and fear of falling trees
long past, he was too lean to cook for now, and
Hope loved a big family, the Methodist gathering
of notable cooks on a month's first Saturday
that brought the county in for casseroles and
jello salad, Sylvia's baked beans and
pies as numerous as news of generations
or yesterday, and there she swooped down
with mighty arms and ankle whites, the house dress
habit of a mothering country saint.

These were Stub's own days of peace reclining
with the packing boxes, odd old chairs, a spinning wheel
resurrected from the soot, a sea chest mustered
from the cellar dust defending Hope's relentless urge
to travel on. They must all be ready, for furniture shrinks
with mere temporary use and has paid ahead for further
life, she editorialized from the barn loft door
while on her knees and handing down a rocking chair
as surely as those wondrous arms would minister
a smothering hug or surpassing apple pie.

Stub had harkened to this litany enough
to know his afterlife would likely be as lively
in any new endearing presence as in
his sundry previous homes. In that good faith
he kept trim and ever rested for upcoming
fresh consignment, secure in the affection
of his next heavenly host.

A Nice Line

That red and blue striped shirt and ironed jeans is Danny
running off to second grade this morning, smiling with the wind.

That shirt, those pants and socks, those pure white undershorts
have flown the line from porch to apple tree all summer long,

secure in his mother's mighty clothespins, practicing
in many a morning's breeze the forward lean required of boys.

She hangs a nice line, it's said in town, almost a kind of
script that he might read, for he is ready to be eight.

Yesterday mid-afternoon it was he took them from the line
himself — the shirt, those pants, a pair of socks,

undershorts on top already mother-smart
to further carry on the drying of a boy behind the ears.

So there goes Danny of the second grade in his red
and blue striped shirt and ironed jeans, sprinting

toward the school bell like the tilting cursive
syllables on the run beneath his tumbling hair.

April's Letter

This is to say nothing
is new. Greetings need substance
to pass on, events witnessed, sights
gathered into cold eyes
and sent off in the mail
like pressed flowers.

Late snow flakes make
poor flowers. The pungence of ice
lingers in a chill-stuck nose, prolongs
the pay for patience, for warmth. So cancel
the need. Dowse
the fires. Draw your feet up and return
to thought. Heat costs
too much. Lack of heat costs
more yet. Move little.
Wait.

Cold steals in
the cracked window sill and runs
loose above the floor, ignorant
of latches. It snakes around me
as if I had on skirts, no socks,
bare legs. Terrible
to be a woman in winter. Then a woman
told me that very thing made the Scots
the fiercest fighters
in the world. But I
would rather not be that fierce
inside my own walls. Besides,
April has never been beaten, and that
is nothing new.
A postcard arrives, spelled out

with distant lands, so peach-lit and easy green
and warm they weaken my knees
and make them sit. Those knees are far away and
don't need news, just something
a little soft from which to pray
or make love. I envy
such simple need, how well
they wait.

The neighbor's one-eyed dog
limps to the granite post. I marvel
he still lifts the good leg. Old age
is not allowed. One unpracticed turn
and you're pissing upwind.

In the sodden woods
a frog croaks, rasped
and bewildered, as if his toes had slipped
from beneath the bed covers. This is not new,
nor that amidst the noise an uncaged rivulet
attacks and smothers a lonesome
snow drift.

I will stay
less fierce this April. I gain
relief if not great warmth
at the granite post. I have learned to croak
at the sun hung limpid
in the gray forenoon, draw my toes back
under the blanket, witness the snowdrift shrink
before the ambush: "But I am on my knees
to make you smile," gurgles the freshet,
barely born. Nothing new. The want of heat
costs more yet, and I can't wait. Got to move
to stay warm.

A Tramp's Odyssey

Of small wallet and bedroll tote, I carry only
this wooden box with hasp and hook an apple orchard man
said I might keep, having slept three nights beside his trees.

I wrote his name on it and carried it ever after
under my arm, enough for the odd few tools of road or rail,
marking the here and there where I stopped to rest.

A tramp can't remember much of a world that gets
so quickly different, I admit, and as I was weary
at the end of days, I took to carving a line with my jackknife

because the words wore thin with my shoes, forgetting
where I might have started out and gone since.
Memory likes sorrow anyway, and forgetting

is God's everyday smile, so my lines cut
gladly parallel and criss-crossed, wondrous
and more mine, a wanderer's map of a place

and its weather, a soul's slim symmetry
of days in the walking rhythm of a hymn overheard
without its prayer, just the simpler marks

from behind my ribs not out to improve upon
a troubled world. I checkered a journey
without beginning or end, ever crossing back

and forth. Soon I grew trim with my cuts—
no more was it a whittled thing—and I carved a border
along the wood where the sundry spirits

marked our kindred hour, a stone in a field
at its haphazard rest, erratic wanderer as I, etched
with its own north and south, a buckled barn

sending its roof-line shadow across my noon
near two lean trees dividing the sky, much as I
have carved my lines in plain and even grain.

Antique Nails

Bless the eyes that they see
only from within, dressing eternity
forever young, contagious
in its beauty, infecting a ripe soul
with fresh joys.

Hope or fact or distant memory -
it's all the same. The eye doesn't
look back at itself.

An old man sitting
in a threadbare chair, rocking
in reverie, looks out through the window
at birds.

He doesn't see the antique nails
rusting through the clapboard paint.

Elegie from Ballyclare

In their 14's in 1908 father and John McKinstrey
kicked a rugby ball all day or ran a scythe
where the hay crept close to the apple trees
at Henryfield Farm.

The two remembered in '53. "Willie, your letter
brought the tear to my eyes. We have not been
happy as 45 years ago. People put it down
to two wars, but you have not forgotten

the family table, my brothers Willie and Sam,
old Andy McKinstry who still worked with us,
Jim Woods and Willie McMeekin,
the Barton's of Larne.

And for the girls that spent their fair time at the farm,
Aggie Dauther, Bella Keton, Lily McKellan,
and never forgetting Aggie Wilson. They are gone
and old Mrs. Strachan now five years.

There came a dryness to the table then.
Father died in '21, mother after 13 weeks,
the shock too much, in 10 years brother Willie.
That left only Sam and me,

so I had to look for a wife and I married a neighbor
which could not be surpassed, had two sons,
one dead at 8, the other that manages the farm
called Samuel after my brother.

As for myself, I am getting along in years
and am got a bit stiffened up, I suppose
I need not complain and hoping this
finds you well, truly yours, John."

That '53 at my own 14, my football still
was at odds with father's Irish foot, but he
showed me how to run a scythe to the apple trees.
Twenty years gone, a frost in October

cut close to his knees. "I guess that's close
enough," he said, a day or two short of 79
and supposing he had no need to complain,
for he had not forgotten Aggie Wilson.

Communion

I try your language, *Domine*,
but *indignus* sum gets me only
a swallow of wine, a wafer, and air too hard
to pray through.

I search Rome's ruins
for relic parts of speech. I find
sum's mirror in verbs ending in *-mus*.
I and we look at each other
across the conjugational divide, spirits arranged
and ready, should a verb come along
looking for a rider or a game of joining
and taking ourselves back, the tensed ping
and pong of pronouns.

It starts with a genteel
back and forth of strokes, then the first
devilish spin close to the net, then a deadly
slam to the opposite corner. I am not,
nor are we, just sportsmen playing
for points of pride. There's a game of spirit
going on here.

I am comfortable enough
in my pronoun, as are you and he and she.
But plurals have no need for identity protection.
I can huddle with others, move en masse,
when it doesn't matter any more
who any of us is. We just
hustle any verb to come down the street
for the promise it holds out, shouting
gaudeamus! at a parading army of stars
and its inscrutable General.

But don't assume I'll fit, Sir,
into one of your constellations. My dignity is quite intact,
and I still dress neatly, if only partly, in my pronoun. It is
my permission to meet with any present tensed long-legged verb
discreetly in the crowd. If I vanish, ascending
in the spin or forehand of desire, I seek only
a redeeming game, even if the outcome
does not bind.

For as it is in a beginning and ever shall be,
even the most singular word still gallops
alone and insufficient towards the treasure
of forgiveness in your smile, and that is
not enough, *Domine*, for the air
so close to earth.

Indignus sum—too little too late. My pronoun
leaps over the divide to multiply the hands
that dig warm dirt, weed and hoe the spirit's leaf,
and praise the creatures here below
from whom all blessings flow.

—Gaudeamus!

His parents both from Maine, Richard Taylor grew up in rural New Hampshire. His education came from Dartmouth, the University of Kiel (Fulbright Fellowship) and Yale. He has been a teacher of German language and literature in colleges, Latin and English as well at private secondary schools. A member of the 1964 Olympic Nordic Ski Team and for many years a staff coach with the National Team, he has been variously a construction worker, ski touring center designer and operator, a translator, and for twenty years (through 2007) a teacher of German, Latin, and English and a running and cross-country ski coach at Gould Academy in Bethel, Maine. He and his wife Sally still live in Bethel. His first book, *The Absence of Strangers,* was published by **Goose River Press** in 2017.

www.ingramcontent.com/pod-product-compliance
Lightning Source LLC
Chambersburg PA
CBHW060534080526
44586CB00012B/729